OBOE & PIANO ACCOMPANIMENT (+ OBOE PART) • PIANO SOLO

GABRIEL'S OBOE

FROM THE MOTION PICTURE

THE MISSION

T0099458

BMG

CHRYSALIS

MUSIC BY
ENNIO MORRICONE

EXCLUSIVELY DISTRIBUTED BY
HAL•LEONARD® CORPORATION
7777 W. BLUEMOUND RD. P.O. BOX 13819 MILWAUKEE, WI 53213

GABRIEL'S OBOE

MUSIC BY ENNIO MORRICONE

Copyright © 1986 BMG VM Music Ltd.
All Rights Administered by BMG Rights Management (US) LLC
All Rights Reserved Used by Permission

PIANO ACCOMPANIMENT (+ OBOE PART)

GABRIEL'S OBOE

FROM THE MOTION PICTURE

THE MISSION

MUSIC BY
ENNIO MORRICONE

BMG
CHRYSALIS

EXCLUSIVELY DISTRIBUTED BY
HAL•LEONARD®
CORPORATION
7777 W. BLUEMOUND RD. P.O. BOX 13819 MILWAUKEE, WI 53213

PIANO
ACCOMPANIMENT

GABRIEL'S OBOE

MUSIC BY ENNIO MORRICONE

Copyright © 1986 BMG VM Music Ltd.
All Rights Administered by BMG Rights Management (US) LLC
All Rights Reserved Used by Permission

poco più mosso
D
A7sus4/E
A7/E
D/F♯
G
A/G
D/F♯
G/F♯
17
mp
mp
E7sus4
A
D
D/C♯
Bm
Bm/A
Gmaj7
G
21
poco cresc.
poco cresc.
D
D/C♯
Bm
Bm/A
Gmaj7
A/G
Dmaj7/F♯
poco rit.
Gadd9
Asus4
A
25
poco dim.
poco dim.
molto rit.
F♯/A♯
4fr
Bm
Bm/A
Gadd9
A9sus4
A
G/D
D
29
pp

poco più mosso
D
A7sus4/E
A7/E
D/F♯
G
A/G
D/F♯
17
mp
G/F♯
E7sus4
A
D
D/C♯
Bm
Bm/A
20
poco cresc.
poco rit.
Gmaj7
G
D
D/C♯
Bm
Bm/A
Gmaj7
A/G
Dmaj7/F♯
Gadd9
24
molto rit.
Asus4
A
F♯/A♯
4fr
Bm
Bm/A
Gadd9
A9sus4
A
G/D
D
28
poco dim.
pp

OBOE

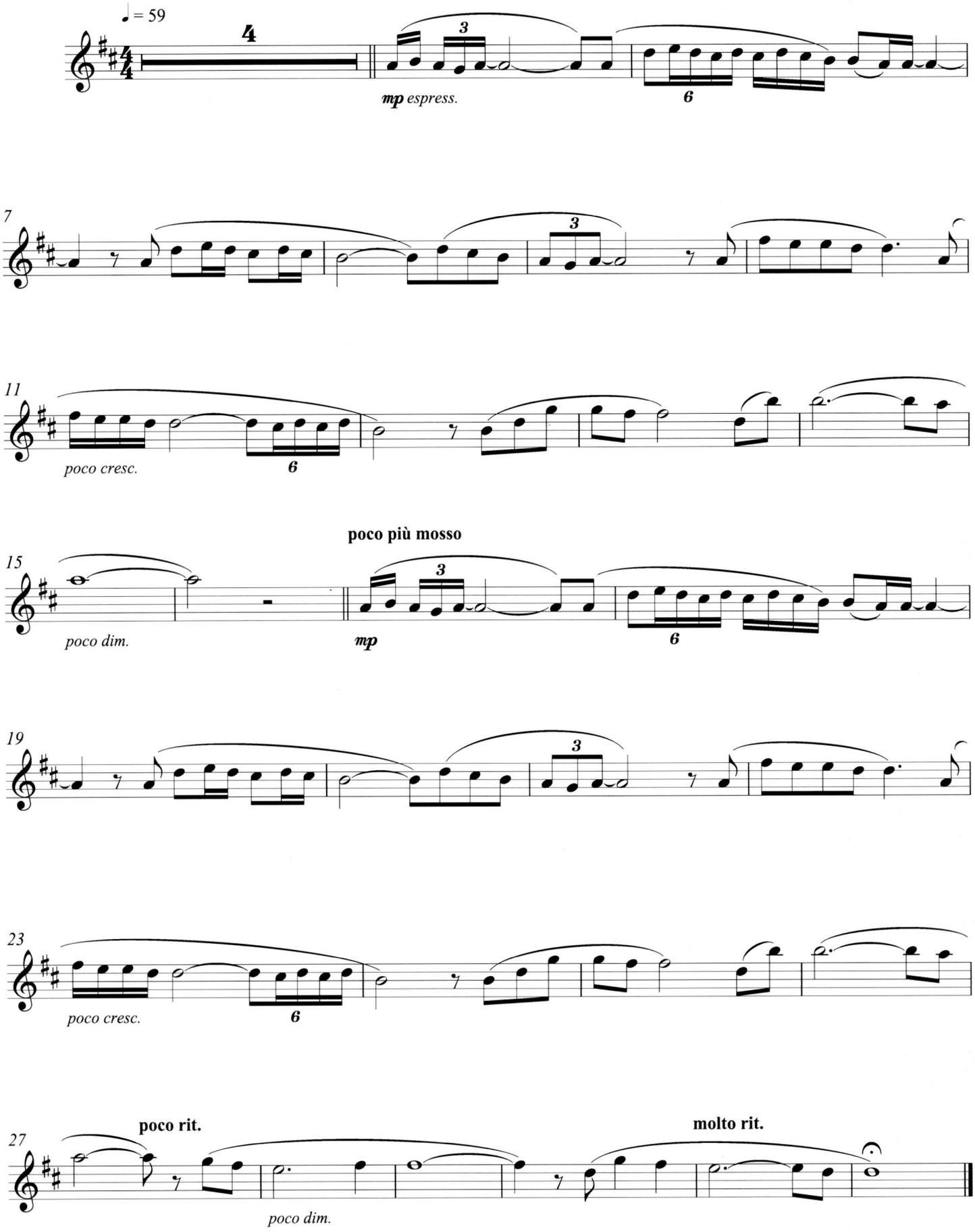

HL00148815

Visit Hal Leonard Online at
www.halleonard.com

U.S. $8.99